We Prepare for
RECONCILIATION

In following Jesus, you discover
the ways of God, and you find a special joy:
the joy of God's love and forgivness.

Authors

Françoise Darcy-Berube
and Jean-Paul Berube

Editors

Gwen Costello
and Myrtle Power

**TWENTY-THIRD
PUBLICATIONS**

**Sacramental Preparation Resources, 3rd edition
We Prepare for Reconciliation
We Share in the Eucharist**

NOVALIS

Nihil Obstat
Caroline Altpeter IBVM
Archdiocese of Toronto
19 June 2009

Imprimatur
+Thomas Collins
Archbishop of Toronto
1 July 2009

Liturgical Advisor: Rev. William Burke, Director, National Liturgy Office
(English Sector), Canadian Conference of Catholic Bishops

© 2019 Novalis Publishing Inc.

Cover: Céleste Gagnon

Design & Layout: Céleste Gagnon

Illustrations: Art Plus: pp. 1, 4, 5, 44, 45, 47; Jocelyne Bouchard: p. 23; June Bradford:
pp. 17, 24, 25, 27, 30, 31; Heather Collins: pp. 40, 41, 42, 43, 48; Suzanne Mogensen:
pp. 6, 32, 33, 54, 55; Anna Payne-Krzyzanowski: cover, pp. 4, 5, 6, 10, 11, 12, 13, 15, 19, 20, 21, 28, 29, 34, 36, 38, 39, 40,
46, 47, 49, 50, 51, 52, and icons.

Photo credits: Page 3: Right: © Jacek Chabraszewski/Dreamstime.com; Page 7: © WP Wittman Photography; Page
8: © Morgan Lane Photography/Shutterstock; Page 9: © iStockphoto.com/Carmen Martínez Banús; Page 10: ©
iStockphoto.com/Pathathai Chungyam; Page 11: © Felix Mizioznikov/Shutterstock; Page 14: Bottom left: © iStockphoto.
com/ Doug Schneider; Page 14: Bottom right: © iStockphoto.com/Yenwen Lu; Page 15: Bottom left: © iStockphoto.
com/Rich Legg; Page 15: Centre: © iStockphoto.com/Özgür Donmaz; Page 15: Top right: © iStockphoto.com/Leah-
Anne Thompson; Page 16: Left: © WP Wittman Photography; Page 16: Right: © Jacek Chabraszewski/Dreamstime.
com; Page 18: © Marzanna Syncerz/Dreamstime.com; Page 22: 2009 © Geo Martinez. Image from BigStockPhoto.
com; Page 26: © iStockphoto.com/ RonTech2000; Page 28: 2009 © Edward Mahala. Image from BigStockPhoto.
com; Page 34: © Nic Neish/Shutterstock; Page 35: © R. Gino Santa Maria/Shutterstock; Page 38: 2009 © Cathy
Yeulet. Image from BigStockPhoto.com; Page 39: © 2009 Jupiterimages Corporation/Goodshoot; Page 53: ©
iStockphoto.com/Juan Gabriel Estey; Page 56: © Monkey Business Images/Dreamstime.com.

Publishing Office:
Novalis
1 Eglinton Avenue East, Suite 800
Toronto, ON, Canada
M4P 3A1

Tel: 416-363-3303   Toll-Free: 1-877-702-7773
Fax: 416-363-9409   Toll-Free: 1-877-702-7775
E-mail: resources@novalis.ca
www.novalis.ca

ISBN 978-2-89688-669-2 (Novalis)
Cataloguing in Publication is available from Library and Archives Canada.

We acknowledge the support of the Government of Canada.

Published in the United States by
Twenty-Third Publications
A Division of Bayard
One Montauk Ave., Suite 200
New London, CT 06320
Tel: 860-437-3012   Toll-Free: 1-800-321-0411
www.twentythirdpublications.com

ISBN: 978-1-62785-454-2 (Twenty-Third Publications)
Library of Congress Control Number: 2019936388

Printed in Canada

Head Office:
4475 Frontenac Street
Montreal, QC, Canada
H2H 2S2

5 4 3 2 1   24 23 22 21 20

Order extra activities for children free of charge at
twentythirdpublications.com in the FREE E-Resources section

Table of Contents

A Special Invitation

Dear Child,

How would you like to go on a wonderful journey, one that will take you closer to God?

A journey like this can be hard at times, but when you stay on it, you will find the path to God.

God, who gives you life, will also give you love, joy, peace, and forgiveness.

On this wonderful journey, you will prepare for the sacrament of forgiveness, which is also called "reconciliation".

If you are ready to begin, just sign your name below.

_____

My First Reconciliation

I will celebrate the sacrament of Reconciliation for the first time on

_____
(Date)

at

_____
(Name of my church)

_____   _____
(My pastor's name)   (My teacher's name)

Signatures of people who helped me prepare for my First Reconciliation

_____

_____

_____

A memory of my special day

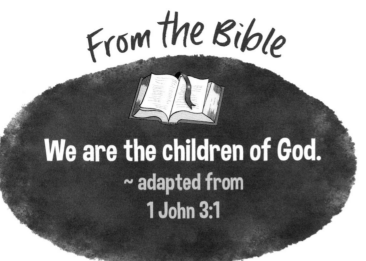

We are the children of God.
~ adapted from
1 John 3:1

Your Journey Begins

All around the world, thousands of boys and girls have begun this **journey**. They are hoping to find new life and to share God's love, joy, peace, and forgiveness. They, like you, are preparing to celebrate the **sacrament** of **Reconciliation** for the first time.

See how excited and happy they are. Where are you in this picture?

Here I am!

You were first invited to walk on the path to God when your parents presented you for **baptism**. You were probably very young then.

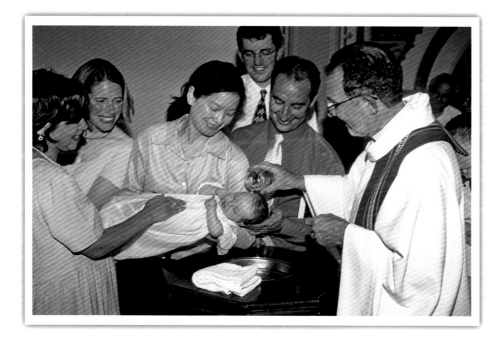

Now that you are older, you can understand better what baptism means. It means you belong to God's family. You are a member of the Church. You are a child of God.

The sacrament of baptism is the first step on the journey of faith. Baptism points the way to God.
– adapted for children from Catechism of the Catholic Church (CCC) #1253

Words to Remember...

Journey ~ a special trip that you need to prepare for with care

Sacraments ~ seven great church celebrations in which Jesus touches our lives

Reconciliation ~ a sacrament that celebrates God's forgiveness in a special way

Baptism ~ the first sacrament, which joins us to the family of God and prepares us to celebrate the other sacraments, especially the Eucharist

1. God Gives You Life

Let us Pray

Here is a beautiful way to praise God. The Church has used this prayer for hundreds of years. When you say it, remember that you are praying with other believers all over the world. Say it often and try to remember it.

Life is wonderful and amazing! To see its beauty, you must open wide your eyes and your heart. Life is a gift from God.

Look around you. See the sky and the sun. You may see flowers, animals, fish, and birds. You may see snowflakes. At nighttime, look at the moon and the stars. All of these are gifts from God.

Glory to the Father,
and to the Son,
and to the Holy Spirit:
as it was in the beginning,
is now,
and will be forever.
Amen.

Life – how great it is! How beautiful! Through days and nights, through summer, fall, winter, and spring, God helps life to change and grow.

See if you can unscramble the sentence below:

NKTAH UOY DGO ROF EHT FGIT FO FELI!

Did you know? God asks YOU to care for the life that fills our world. What can you do today to care for God's gifts?

Today I can

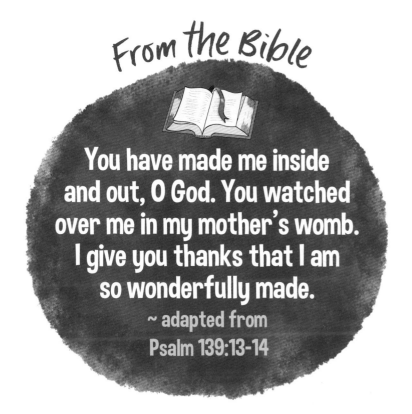

You have made me inside and out, O God. You watched over me in my mother's womb. I give you thanks that I am so wonderfully made.

~ adapted from Psalm 139:13-14

You Are Fully Alive!

It's amazing what you can do because you are alive. You can do things you don't even think about, like breathing, seeing, moving, and jumping.

Here are ways to think about how you are fully alive.

1. Sit down in a chair and put your hands on your lap. Close your eyes and take deep **breaths** three or four times. Then sit very still and listen to your heartbeat. Do you hear it?

2. Feel the air entering your body and giving it life. Then say out loud, "My voice, too, is a gift from God."

3. Smile a big smile and then open your eyes. Slowly stand up, raise your arms, and start moving them all around. Kick your feet up and down.

See all that you can do! Isn't it wonderful to be alive?

Of all the things you can do because God has made you fully alive, which four things can you do best?

1. _____

2. _____

3. _____

4. _____

God made you the way you are. Here is what God says about you in the Bible:

From the Bible

You are beautiful in my eyes. I love you. I have called you by your name. You are my child!

~ adapted from
Isaiah 45:4

Saint Francis Loved Life

Francis lived a very long time ago in Assisi, a little town in the country of Italy. Just like you, Francis wanted to be happy. His father was rich, so he had plenty of food to eat, nice clothes to wear, lots of toys and games to play with, and he had fun with his friends.

When he became a man, Francis knew that deep down in his heart, he was not really happy. One day he walked to an old church and sat down in the quiet space. He felt something tugging at his heart. He felt God speaking to him.

"Yes," Francis thought, "God is calling me to do something more with my life." From then on, he left behind his riches so he could follow Jesus. After that, everything he saw in God's creation filled him with happiness and joy. He cried out, "Praise to you, Lord, for our brother the sun and our sister the moon!"

One day, it is said, Francis even tamed a wild wolf. He said, "Brother wolf, please stop scaring the people. Go back to your forest. You will be happier there." The wolf did just as Francis asked. Little birds would sometimes land on his arm and sing God's praises with Francis. All the animals loved him.

Write here the names of some of your family members and friends.

Let us Pray

If you want to thank God as Francis did, you can say this prayer. When you get to the words "Thank you, God!" shout them out with joy.

For the sun that fills the sky,
for the moon and the stars at night,
Thank you, God!

For the wind in the trees,
for the rain that falls on the earth,
Thank you, God!

For the fish and the birds,
for the animals in the forest,
Thank you, God!

For my family and friends,
for my life and happiness,
Thank you, God!

Make others happy with the gifts God has given you.

~ adapted from
1 Peter 4:10

God Gives You Talents!

Do you know what it means to be **unique**? It means there is no one like you in the whole world – no one. God made you with your own smile, your own face, your own body. God gave you special gifts called **talents**. Your talents are the things you do very well.

There once was a boy named Henry. Many other children lived in his neighbourhood.

There was Momei, who could play the piano and sing.

There was Luis, who could kick a soccer ball farther than anyone.

There was Samuel, who always got the best marks in school.

There was Julie, who could run and jump higher than Henry could.

At first, Henry was jealous of all these talents. Then one day his mother said, "Henry, you are always so kind to everyone. You are a very good friend."

Henry understood that being a good friend was his special talent.

At bedtime he prayed, "Thank you, Jesus, for my special talent."

Something to Think About

- What is your special talent?
- What other talents do you have?
- Are you a good friend like Henry?
- Do you thank God every day for your talents?

The Church Teaches...

Our talents are God's gifts.
- adapted from CCC #2009

Words to Remember...

Breath ~ a gift from God that helps you be fully alive

Praise ~ a way to tell God and others how wonderful they are

Unique ~ one of a kind in all the world

Talents ~ the things you do very well

You Can Talk to God

As you can see, God loves you very much. When you spend time talking to God, you are loving God back. Talking to God is called **prayer**.

Ask your family to help you set up a space in your room or home where you can go to pray. You can call this your "prayer corner." Make it special and beautiful.

In this space, put colourful pictures, a Bible, and anything else that reminds you of God.

In the morning, say, "Good morning, God."

In the evening, say, "Good night, God."

All day long, you can speak to God about whatever you are doing.

You can say, "Dear God, you are great. Thanks so much for all you do."

When you spend time each day talking with God and saying thanks, you will have joy in your heart.

1. What Have You Learned?

Remember what you have learned so far and answer these questions.

Find the answers on the apple tree.

1. I am on a special ____ ____ ____ ____ to God.

2. The first sacrament I received is

   ____ ____ ____ ____ ____ ____ ____ .

3. The ____ ____ ____ ____ ____ ____ ____
   I am preparing for is Reconciliation.

4. Every day God gives me new ____ ____ ____ .

5. Saint Francis often said words of

   ____ ____ ____ ____ ____ ____ .

6. ____ ____ ____ ____ ____ ____ means talking to God.

Things you can do to show your love for God.
- Take good care of the Earth and all that is in it.
- Never harm another creature on purpose.
- Tell God "thanks" when you see something beautiful.
- Take time each day to talk to God about your life.

The Church Teaches...

Prayer means taking time to be alone with God who loves us.
– adapted from CCC #2709

17

2. God Gives You Love

Sit quietly and think about these words. Ask Jesus to help you understand them deep within your heart.

"You shall love the Lord your God with all your heart, and with all your soul, and with all your might, and your neighbour as yourself."

~ adapted from Deuteronomy 6:5 and Mark 12:31

Jesus is the best teacher when it comes to love. Even as a child he studied the Word of God. He learned about the **Law of Love** that God gave to the Jewish people.

While he was growing up, Jesus tried to follow God's Law of Love. Little by little, he found the way to true happiness. It is NOT through riches, or power, or beauty, or being famous. The way to true happiness, Jesus found, is through great love. Jesus spoke about God's love with the people and he showed them how to love others.

If you want to be happy, look for God's love in your life. Open your heart to sharing, forgiving, and helping those in need.

From the Bible

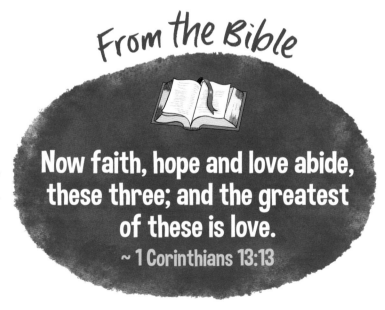

Now faith, hope and love abide, these three; and the greatest of these is love.
~ 1 Corinthians 13:13

A Happy Celebration

One day Jesus came to a town called Capernaum. The people ran to greet him because they had heard about his preaching and healing. Jesus was happy to meet them and tell them about God's love. But the day was hot and in the evening Jesus was very tired. Many sick people were still waiting to see him.

When he saw this, he felt sorry for them. He forgot how tired he was. He took time with each one, blessing them and healing them all.

Imagine the celebration that evening in Capernaum!

Something to Think About

- Why didn't Jesus tell the people, "Come back tomorrow. I'm too tired right now"?
- What would you have done when you saw all those people?
- What do you do now when you are tired but someone needs your help?

One of Jesus' best friends was Peter. He was a fisherman who worked hard to take care of his family. One day Jesus said to him, "Why don't you change jobs? Come and be my helper." Peter liked that idea.

He put down his fishing nets and went with Jesus. He listened and he learned about God's Law of Love.

The Church Teaches...

Be merciful and forgiving, as Jesus was, and love others as he has loved us.
- adapted for children from CCC #2842

"Love one another as I have loved you." This is what Jesus asks us to do.

A few years later, when Jesus was arrested, Peter forgot God's Law of Love. He was afraid that he would be arrested, too. So he told people he didn't know Jesus. He lied! He turned his back on his best friend!

When Peter realized what he had done, he was so ashamed, he ran away crying.

But the story doesn't end there. After God raised Jesus from the dead, Jesus came to see Peter. Jesus didn't get angry at all. He loved Peter and he forgave him. What a relief! Peter and Jesus were **reconciled**, and Peter kept growing in God's love. Soon Peter became the leader of those first followers of Jesus.

Something to Think About

- **Why do you think Jesus forgave Peter?**
- **Would you want Jesus for a friend? Explain your answer.**

Let us Pray

Peter was sorry he had failed Jesus. Maybe Peter said a prayer like this:

Lord Jesus, Son of God, have mercy on me, a sinner.

Following Jesus

Before he returned to his Father in heaven, Jesus told his followers:

> ## "I am giving you a new commandment. Love one another as I have loved you."
>
> ~ John 15:12

But can we really love as Jesus did? Can we forgive as Jesus did? Yes, but only when we open ourselves to God's Law of Love as Jesus did.

Read this story about a boy named Thomas. Was he open to God's Law of Love?

Something to Think About

- What do you think? Did Thomas practise God's Law of Love?
- Would you have done what he did? Why or why not?
- What act of love can YOU do today?

One day at school, Mrs. Perada had a surprise for the class.

A friend had given her a box of candy and she wanted to share it with the children. Everyone took a big bite and said, "Yummy! So delicious!" Everyone but Thomas, that is.

"Don't you like candy?" Mrs. Perada asked him.

"Yes, I do," Thomas said, "but I want to keep it for my little brother, Dylan. He never gets candy."

The teacher said, "It's good of you to think of Dylan, but isn't it hard to give away your own treat?"

"Yes," Thomas answered, "but if I eat it now, it'll feel good in my mouth. If I give it to Dylan, it'll feel even better in my heart."

Saint Damian of Molokai was a **missionary** in Hawaii. He took care of sick people called "lepers" who had been left on the island of Molokai because their disease was contagious. Damian treated the lepers just as he would have treated Jesus. He often took care of their wounds himself. Damian loved these suffering people just as Jesus loved them.

To do good things for others as Jesus, and Thomas, and Saint Damian did, you have to keep your eyes and your heart wide open.

Does someone need your help: your parents, your sisters and brothers, your friends, your schoolmates? If they do, act as Jesus did.

Words to Remember...

Law of Love ~ a way to live that puts God and others first

Reconciled ~ to make things right with God and others when we have done wrong

Commandment ~ a rule in the Bible about how to live

Missionary ~ a person who carries the good news of God's love to all the world

Let us Pray

Lord Jesus, may I care for others as you care for them. May I love those in need as you love them.

Ways to Show Love

You are on a journey that is taking you closer to God. You are on your way to celebrating God's forgiveness in the sacrament of Reconciliation. Before you arrive at this sacrament, you have to practise how to love and forgive.

Read the stories below. What is the best way each child in the stories can show love?

Ned notices that his neighbours Alberto and Rafaela are sad. Alberto is crying.

"Why are you so sad?" Ned asks.

"Our mom just lost her job," Rafaela explained, "and Alberto's birthday is coming soon. He was supposed to have a party and now he can't."

What can Ned do to help? What can his family do?

_____

_____

_____

Emma is playing in the driveway. Her toys are all spread out. Her neighbour Maria calls out, "Come and play with me!" Emma knows that if she leaves her toys where they are, her dad will have to get out of the car and move them when he gets home from work, but she wants to go and play with Maria right away. What will Emma do?

Simon and his friends are playing soccer in the park. Adam is watching from his wheelchair. He wants to play, but he can't run. What will Simon and his friends do?

Eric and Marisol look out the window one day. They see an old woman who lives nearby. She is always walking alone. Today she is carrying two bags of groceries. Eric and Marisol feel sorry for her. They tell their parents about her. How could they help their neighbour?

👁 LOOK AND LISTEN 🔊

Here's a game you can play with your family to help you **SEE** and **HEAR** how to love one another better.

Everyone writes their name on a slip of paper and puts it in a bag. Then they each pick one name out of the bag, without showing it to the others. (If someone picks their own name, they put that slip of paper back and pick again.) For the next week, everyone does secret good deeds for the person whose name they picked. At the end of the week, have everyone try to guess who was doing these loving things for them.

Sharing Family Love

Benjamin is excited. His grandparents are coming for dinner! That means they will all sit at the table for a long time, sharing good food and family stories. "Hurray!" says his sister Michelle. "I love it when we have special meals."

We all love times of celebration. Every family has its own way of celebrating. Family traditions make special days even more special. A tradition is something passed down from grandparents to parents to children: certain actions, certain ways of celebrating, even certain stories that are told just the right way. Family meals are the best time to share your family traditions.

Ask your parents to plan a special meal, a time when you can share love and laughter.

Something to Think About

- Do you enjoy special celebrations and special meals? Why?
- What are your family's traditions?
- What can you SEE and HEAR around your family table?

2. What Have You Learned?

Think about the journey you are on. You have already come a very long way. See what you can remember so far. **HINT** Look at the signs.

1. God gave the Jewish people a L _____ _____ of L _____ _____ _____ .

2. F _____ g _____ e n _____ _____ is the gift Jesus gave to Peter.

3. To make things okay again is also called R _____ _____ on _____ _____ iati _____ _____ .

4. Family meals are a wonderful t _____ _____ d _____ _____ _____ o _____ .

5. Jesus said to his followers: Lo _____ _____ o _____ ano _____ _____ r.

Who said, "Oh no, I have betrayed Jesus"?
HINT His name begins with "P." _____ _____ _____ _____ _____

Who said: "I'm saving it for my little brother"?
HINT His brother's name was Dylan. _____ _____ _____ _____ _____

Who took care of sick people called "lepers" on the island of Molokai?

_____ _____ _____ _____

HINT He was a missionary.

Who said, "I love it when we have special meals"?

HINT Her brother's name was Benjamin.

_____ _____ _____ _____

Love is patient.
Love is kind.
Love does good
things for others!

love one another

Tradition

Law of love

Reconciliation

Forgiveness

27

3. God Gives You Joy

Isn't it great to know how much God loves you? Isn't it a blessing to know that God will always love you and forgive you, no matter what?

When you are loved and forgiven, you feel happy inside. This feeling is called **joy**. Jesus felt joy because he knew God his Father loved him. He talked to God all through his day – every day!

From the Bible

God, you are the joy of my heart!
~ Psalm 104:34

Estella was angry with her mother because she would not allow her to go to Sophia's house with her friends. "You're so unfair," cried Estella. "All the other kids get to go!"

That very day, one of Estella's friends fell and cut her arm at Sophia's house, and no adult was home to take her to the hospital. She was bleeding for a long time. That night Estella told her mother she was sorry for her angry words.

Her mother said, "I understand. It's hard to be left behind, but I want you to be safe. I forgive you for your anger."

Estella felt so relieved. She had a deep feeling of joy in her heart.

We Prepare for
RECONCILIATION

Dear Parents,

You have asked your parish to help you prepare your child for the sacrament of Reconciliation. This is an important step in your child's moral and spiritual development.

A few years ago, you asked for your child to be baptized. The Church gladly welcomed your child and in turn invited you to share your faith with your child.

You have always been for your child the first sign, the first "sacrament" of God's love. It is through the simple gestures of your daily loving care that your child's heart and mind have been opened up to faith and trust in God's infinite tenderness.

Now, with the upcoming celebration of First Reconciliation, you are invited to share in the very special experience of preparing your child—in your own home, at your own pace. No one can do this as well as you can, because no one is closer to your child than you are. Be assured, however, that your parish community will provide support and walk with you on this faith journey.

This Family Guide is intended to help make the journey easy and enjoyable for you and your child.

We hope that the stories and pictures in your child's book will offer you an exciting starting point for one-on-one conversations. You know how much your child appreciates special time with you! We hope that the journey you are about to embark on will be a wonderful faith-enriching experience for you and your child, bringing you even closer to each other and to Jesus, our Lord.

Your Role

Preparing children for the sacrament of Reconciliation involves more than getting them ready for a ceremony. It should also do the following:

- teach them to walk in the path of God's love, which strengthens their self-esteem and at the same time makes it easier for them to accept their personal limitations and shortcomings
- help them discover that Jesus shows them the way to God
- encourage them to develop simple habits of prayer that will sustain their spiritual life while strengthening their character
- enable them to acquire gradually a more precise sense of right and wrong, and make their own moral decisions
- instill in them a deep trust in the infinite love of God, who always forgives them

Our approach

This preparation journey is built on two very important foundations.

1. **Regular conversations with your child**

Spend one-on-one time together discussing and reinforcing what your child is learning. It's easy! Just read a few pages together from your child's book and use the ideas provided to begin your conversations. After reading and talking, do the suggested activities together. When your child has completed an activity, take time to admire what he or she has done. Always share your own comments and reactions.

Good conversations happen in an atmosphere of joy, peace, and prayer. Here are a few ways to create such a mood at home.

- Talk to your child and agree on the best time for your conversations. Stick to the schedule as best you can.
- Choose a place where you won't be disturbed, and ask other family members to give you some privacy.
- Before you begin, light a candle or vigil light to create a prayerful atmosphere. Share a moment of silence together to become aware of God's presence. Then pray a short prayer, such as: "Dear God, be with us as we talk." or "Give us your joy and love, dear God."

2. **Special attention to your child's daily life and prayer**

This journey of preparing for First Reconciliation is an intense time. Your child will learn what it means to be a Christian, a follower of Jesus Christ. You will want to be extra attentive to your child's positive and negative experiences, so you can discuss them and reflect on them together. This doesn't mean that you should be more critical of your child. Just the opposite! A child needs encouragement just as a plant needs water. Encourage your child to put into practice what he or she discovers at each step on this journey.

This journey also offers a good opportunity to develop the habit of daily prayer, which is important for your child's whole life. At the centre of this guide you will find six prayer cards, one for each of the five themes in your child's book plus one for immediate preparation for the sacrament. Set aside some prayer time each day. (Remember: this means praying with your child, not just listening to your child's prayers.) Cut out the prayers and give one to your child at the beginning of each theme. Read the prayers together morning and evening. You may wish to invite other family members to join you. Help your child set up his or her prayer corner: a space where he or she can pray with some privacy. In the prayer corner, place a Bible, a picture of Jesus or pictures your child has drawn, and a candle. Add other objects as your child continues on this journey of preparation.

Special note: *The prayer cards all offer themes of peace, thanksgiving, and reconciliation, which in turn reflect the themes in the liturgy. The whole message of the Gospel is reconciliation, and all liturgy is about reconciliation.*

Celebrating the start of the journey

Once your child begins this journey, have a meal to celebrate. Invite grandparents, godparents, and close friends from the parish. Serve a special dessert. During the meal, give your child a card signed by all present with thoughts and blessings for a "happy journey to First Reconciliation." Take time at this meal to tell family members that you will be having regular private conversations with your child as he or she prepares.

(Ideally, both parents will be part of this journey and will be involved as much as possible throughout the year.)

Preparing for each theme

There are five themes (or chapters) in your child's book. Before starting a new theme, take time to read everything related to that theme in your child's book and in this Family Guide. The themes flow from one to the next in order. The points made in each theme are important to what follows, so make sure you do each one.

1. God Gives You Life

Goals

- **to help your child see life as a gift from God**
- **to awaken in your child's heart gratitude for the gift of life**
- **to encourage your child to share his or her gifts and talents with others**

(Before you begin, gather some mementoes from your child's birth or baptism: photos, a baptismal candle or robe, cards or letters you have saved. If possible, buy a small plant for your child's prayer corner.)

Parent/child conversations

Pages 4, 5, 6 and 7 *(These page numbers and the pages that follow under "Parent/child conversations" refer to the pages in your child's book.)*

- Set a prayerful tone for your first conversation. This will set the tone for all the others. Take time to get settled. Invite your child to light the candle. Share a moment of silence to become aware of God's presence.
- Read the letter on page 4 of your child's book. Share your thoughts about being invited to parties, games, etc. How is this invitation the same or different? Be sure your child understands that he or she will be preparing for First Reconciliation before signing page 4.
- Read pages 6 and 7 together. Take time to describe your child's birth and baptism. Emphasize how happy you were to welcome this new member of your family. Then share together the photos and mementoes you have gathered.
- Discuss together the "Words to Remember" on page 7. Be sure your child can define each one in his or her own words.

Pages 8 and 9

- Read pages 8 and 9 together and talk about the living creatures in the photos. (If you bought a plant, now might be the time to give it to your child and explain how to care for it.)
- Unscramble the sentence on Page 9 and say it together as a prayer.

Pages 10 and 11

- Share the three ways your child can be fully alive from page 10. Do the actions together. Help your child complete the list on page 11.
- Pray together the Bible verse on page 11. Tell your child, "This is what God thinks of you."

Pages 12, 13, 14 and 15

- Read pages 12 and 13 and talk about St. Francis. What does your child like most about his story? Read the "Let us Pray" prayer and shout out "Thank you, God!" together.
- Read Henry's story on pages 14 and 15. Discuss the "Something to Think About" questions. Go over the "Words to Remember" and be sure your child can define them in his or her own words.
- Share the "From the Bible" words on page 14. Ask your child how he or she might do this action.

Pages 16 and 17

- Read page 16 together. This important page will help your child to develop the habit of daily prayer. To make prayer a part of everyday life, however, your child needs your constant encouragement.
- Take time to do the activities on page 17. Review the things your child can do to show love for God. Share ways that you try to do the same.

Suggestions for daily life

- Talk about your child's prayer corner. Is it working or does it need some tweaking? Is your child using it for prayer? Why or why not?
- Focus on your child's special talents and offer encouragement for developing them.

Enrichment activities

- Visit the library and find and read together an illustrated story about St. Francis of Assisi.
- After Mass, talk about your church as a place of prayer. Walk around with your child and look at pictures, statues, the altar, the candles. What ideas can your child incorporate in his or her prayer corner?

2. God Gives You Love

- to help your child understand that the message to "Love one another" is at the heart of Christian living
- to give your child the opportunity to discover the joy of loving in daily life, even when love calls for sacrifice

Parent/child conversations

Pages 18, 19, 20 and 21

- Read God's Law of Love on page 18 ("You shall love the Lord your God …"). Have your child repeat it after you line by line three times.
- Read together and talk about the gospel story on page 19 and discuss the "Something to Think About" questions.
- Share the story about Peter on pages 20 and 21. Explain to your child that Jesus invited Peter to learn God's Law of Love. Even when Peter failed, Jesus forgave him. Pray together the prayer of contrition on page 21 of your child's book under "Let us Pray."

Pages 22, 23, 24 and 25

- Read the story about Thomas on page 22 and discuss the "Something to Think About" questions on page 22.
- Talk about Saint Damian and his work (page 23). Go over the "Words to Remember" and be sure your child can define them.
- Share the stories on pages 24 and 25 and talk about them together. If you have time, plan how you will do the "Look and Listen" activity on page 25. Involve the whole family, if possible.

Pages 26 and 27

- Read page 26 together and talk about your own family situation. Ask your child for ideas for a special meal to celebrate being a family. Then discuss the "Something to Think About" questions.
- Help your child complete the sentences on page 27, and then see if he or she remembers the "Who Said" answers.

Suggestions for daily life

- When questions about right and wrong come up, instead of first giving your own answer, invite your child to reflect and to think of Jesus' example. You might ask your child: *"What do you think? Why would you do this and not that? What do you think Jesus would do?"*
- Using daily events as examples, help your child to be aware of the joy he or she experiences by living God's Law of Love, even when doing so is difficult. Encourage your child to share this joy and to give thanks for it.

Enrichment activities

- Invite your family to think about ways you can share meals more often. Then choose a time to discuss this subject seriously. What suggestions can you put into practice right away? Family meals are a time for bonding, for conversation, for celebrating the joys of family life, for sharing daily burdens with one another and for passing on family traditions.
- Plan a family meal (prepared with your child) to celebrate family life. Choose a date or occasion that is meaningful to your family. Invite extended family members and ask them to recall family stories they can share with your child.

God Gives Us Life

Parent: Remember that God's love gives us life. Here is God's message for us today.

(If you have a family Bible, show it to your child before reading this verse, to help him or her recognize these as special words: God's Word.)

> You are precious in my sight, and I love you.
>
> –Isaiah 43:4

Child: Thank you, God, for loving me so much.

Parent: God will walk with us today in all that we do.

Child: Thank you, God, for watching over me.

Parent: Let us now share a sign of our faith in God...

Parent/Child: In the name of the Father,
and of the Son,
and of the Holy Spirit.
Amen.

Parent: Let us remember that God is always with us, when we are awake and when we are asleep. Let us now listen to God's message for us this evening.

> It is I, your God, who made the earth. I made all the creatures who live on the earth. It is I who made the sky and the stars.
>
> –adapted from Jeremiah 32:13

Child: Dear God, thank you for the gifts of the earth.

Parent: God, you have created such wonderful things for us. We thank you with all our hearts.

Parent/Child: For the sun and moon,
for the wind in the trees,
for the fish and the birds
and all animals...
Thank you, God.
Amen.

(Now trace the sign of the cross on your child's forehead.)

God Gives Us Love

Parent: Remember that God's love will be with us all day. Let us listen together to God's Word and keep it in our hearts.

> My love for you will never end.
> I have always loved you, and I always will.
>
> –Jeremiah 31:3

Child: Dear God, I am so happy that you love me.

Parent: God does wonderful things for us every day; holy is God's name.

Child: Help me to think of you often today, holy God.

Parent: Let us praise God together …

Parent/Child: Glory to the Father,
and to the Son
and to the Holy Spirit.
As it was in the beginning,
is now,
and will be forever.
Amen.

Parent: Let us take time now to talk to God before we go to sleep. *(Pause for a few seconds)* God is with us at all times. Here is God's message for us this evening …

> Do not be afraid, for I am with you.
>
> –Genesis 26:24

Child: Thank you, God, for being with me tonight.

Parent: Lord, watch over us and fill us with your peace and joy.

Child: Thank you, God, for putting your joy in my heart.

Parent: Let us now pray to God our Father …

Parent/Child: Our Father, who art in heaven,
hallowed be thy name;
thy kingdom come,
thy will be done on earth
as it is in heaven.
Amen.

(Now trace the sign of the cross on your child's forehead.)

God Gives Us Joy

In the Morning

Parent: Remember that God fills our hearts with joy. Here is God's message of joy for us today.

> God's love has been poured into our hearts through the Holy Spirit.
> –Romans 5:5

Child: Dear God, fill my heart with your love and joy.

Parent: Let us pray together that God will walk with us in all we do today.

Parent/Child: Dear God, here we are,
giving thanks for this day.
With Jesus, your Son,
we give you all that we do.
We give you our love, too,
and with Jesus we pray,
"May your kingdom come."
Amen.

In the Evening

Parent: Thank you, God, for all the times we felt joy today. Please watch over us tonight as we think about your Bible words.

> Make a joyful noise to God, all the earth!
> –Psalm 66:1

Child: Dear Jesus, I want to be your friend always.

Parent: Let us now talk to God about our day: what gave us joy and what was difficult.

(Pause for a few seconds)

Parent/Child: You have been with us in everything we did today. Thank you, God.

(Now trace the sign of the cross on your child's forehead.)

God Gives Us Peace

Parent: Remember today that the Spirit of Jesus is with us to help us share peace with everyone we meet. Here is God's Word for us today.

Parent: Let us take time now to speak to Jesus about our day: our joys and difficulties and the times we felt God's peace. *(Pause for a few seconds)* Let us remember his words.

> Happy are the peacemakers; they are truly the children of God.
>
> –Matthew 5:8-10

> Peace I leave with you; my peace I give you.
>
> –John 14:27

Child: Dear Jesus, help me to have peace in my heart today.

Parent: Help us to make peace with anyone who has hurt us.

Child: Walk with me today, dear Jesus, in all that I do.

(Now share a sign of peace.)

Parent/Child: May the peace of Christ be with you. And with your spirit.

Child: Thank you, God, for the peace of this day.

Parent: If we have failed to offer peace today, please forgive us.

Child: Forgive me, dear God, if I hurt others today.

Parent: Let us pray now as Jesus taught us …

Parent/Child: Give us this day our daily bread; and forgive us our trespasses as we forgive those who trespass against us. Amen.

(Now trace the sign of the cross on your child's forehead.)

God Gives Us Forgiveness

Parent: Let us remember today that Jesus, our Good Shepherd, will be with us in all that we do.

Child: Thank you, Jesus, for watching over me.

Parent: Here are Jesus' words from the Bible for us today.

> There will be joy in heaven over one sinner who repents.
>
> –Luke 15:7

Child: Dear Jesus, forgive me for my sins.

Parent: Let us pray to Jesus together.

Parent/Child: Lord Jesus, you are our Good Shepherd.
You are always with us,
so we will not be afraid.
Thank you for keeping us on
the path to God.
Amen.

Parent: Let us remember that Jesus has walked with us today.

Child: Thank you, Jesus, for being with me.

Parent: Let us listen together to God's Word to us this evening.

> Just as I have loved you, you also should love one another.
>
> –John 13:34

Child: Forgive me, Jesus, if I have not loved others today.

Parent: Let us ask for God's forgiveness together.

Parent/Child: Dear Jesus, we are sorry for doing wrong. We love you and do not want to sin again. You are all good and deserving of all our love. We will try with your help to sin no more. Amen.

(Now trace the sign of the cross on your child's forehead.)

God Gives Us Reconciliation

Parent: Let us remember that God has given us the sacrament of Reconciliation, a sign that God always offers us love and forgiveness.

Child: Thank you, God, for this special sacrament.

Parent: When we are truly sorry, we show it by changing our ways and living God's Law of Love.

Child: Help me to love others as you love them, O God.

Parent: Let us listen to God's Word to us today.

> For if you forgive others, your heavenly Father will also forgive you.
>
> –Matthew 6:14

Child: As I prepare for the sacrament of Reconciliation, Jesus, please fill my heart with your love.

Parent: May peace be in your heart as you prepare.

(Now share a sign of peace.)

Parent: As the time draws near for your First Reconciliation, I ask God to bless you with peace, joy, and forgiveness.

Child: Open my heart to your Law of Love, O God.

Parent: I ask God to open your heart to receive forgiveness.

Child: Open my heart to your forgiveness, O God.

Parent: I ask God to open your heart to this message.

> You shall love the Lord your God with all your heart, soul, and mind, and you shall love your neighbour as yourself.
>
> –Matthew 22:34-39

Parent: Thank you for the gift of the sacrament of Reconciliation, loving God. Bless my child as he/she prepares to receive it.

(Now trace the sign of the cross on your child's forehead.)

3. God Gives You Joy

- to help your child understand that God lives in his or her heart
- to awaken in your child the desire to pray

Parent/child conversations

Pages 28, 29, 30 and 31

- Read together pages 28 and 29, and talk about Estella's story. Then share the "From the Bible" words and discuss them with your child. Discuss the "Something to Think About" questions.

- Read together the words of the Lord's Prayer, also called the Our Father, on pages 30 and 31. Ask your child what each phrase means to him or her, then share the explanations on these pages. Close by praying the Our Father together.

Pages 32 and 33

- Read together how Connor, Rosa, Mario, and Simon try to pray. Then talk about how we pray at Mass and the importance of participating fully through our prayers, singing, and sharing in the Lord's Supper. Though your child can't yet participate at communion time, discuss the term "the Lord's Supper" and what it means to you.

Pages 34, 35 and 36

- Try "quiet prayer" with your child, perhaps in your child's prayer corner. Go through each step and then talk about this experience. Encourage your child to pray this way often. If you have time, also pray the "imagination prayer." Which does your child prefer? Why? Which works best for you?

- Read page 36 together, then say the Hail Mary slowly and reverently. Encourage your child to memorize this prayer (and the Our Father) before First Reconciliation.

Page 37

- Invite your child to answer the three questions on this page and discuss them. Also go over the "Words to Remember" and be sure your child can define them in his or her own words.

- Talk about the suggested ways to keep God's joy in your heart. Focus in particular on your child's prayer corner as a place for him or her to talk to God. End by holding hands and praying the Our Father.

Suggestions for daily life

- Choose one of the Bible quotations from this theme and write it on a piece of paper.

- Have your child decorate it, place it in his or her prayer corner, and recite it daily.

- At the end of each day, share with your child a thought or prayer that you have experienced and invite your child to do the same with you.

Enrichment activities

- At least once a week, practise "silent prayer" together. Invite family members to join you.

- Before Mass each week, remind your child that this is a very special way to pray. It is "community" prayer because we all come together to praise God and celebrate the presence of Jesus among us.

4. God Gives You Peace

- to help your child understand that we all sometimes fail to follow God's paths
- to awaken in your child's heart the confidence that God always forgives us

Parent/child conversations

Pages 38, 39, 40, 41, 42 and 43

- Read together and talk about pages 38 and 39, especially the concept of sin. How does your child understand sin? Talk about the stories on pages 40, 41, 42 and 43 and reflect with your child on the consequences of the behaviours of the children in the stories. Ask your child if any of these situations are familiar. What did he or she think and feel when it happened to them?

- Be sure your child understands the text at the bottom of page 39. Use concrete examples to show the difference between an error or mistake (not done on purpose) and a sin (something we do on purpose that turns us away from God and hurts others).

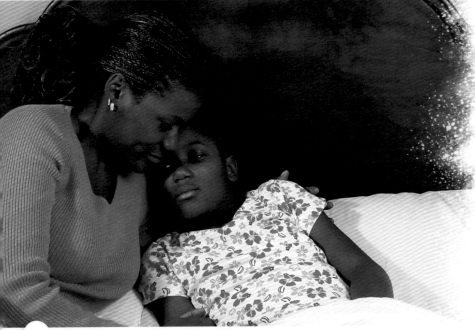

Pages 44, 45, 46 and 47

- Read pages 44 and 45 and talk about having a "conscience." To know right from wrong, your child's conscience has to be "informed." (One way to inform our conscience is to get advice from the Bible and Church teachings.) Share some of these "rules" from pages 44 and 45 with your child: the Ten Commandments as well as teachings from Jesus.

- Read together pages 46 and 47. Take time to talk about the questions on page 47 and invite your child to answer them. Talk about your own experiences of being forgiven, and end by praying together the "Let us Pray" prayer.

Pages 48 and 49

- Read together and discuss the sentences on page 48 and help your child to complete them. Then carefully review the "Words to Remember" on page 49. Be sure your child can define them in his or her own words.

Suggestions for daily life

- Using examples from your child's own life, help her or him to become aware of when something is his or her own fault. Encourage your child to ask forgiveness from God and others, and then make a gesture of reconciliation to set things right. Avoid labelling your child's behaviour as "sinful." Sin comes from the heart, and only your child can know whether an act is truly sinful.

- If your child has done something wrong and wants to talk about it, you can use questions like these: "How do you feel about what you did? Why did you do it? What can you do now to make things better?" Always finish such conversations with words of forgiveness.

Enrichment activities

- Visit your parish church with your child and show him or her the reconciliation room. Talk about the sacrament of Reconciliation and how it brings peace and forgiveness from God.

- Invite your child to accompany you to church when you receive the sacrament of Reconciliation. Your example will speak louder than your words.

5. God Gives You Forgiveness

Goals

- to introduce your child to Jesus as a good shepherd who loves and forgives our sins
- to encourage your child to pray daily for God's guidance
- to help your child prepare more immediately to receive the sacrament of Reconciliation

Parent/child conversations

Pages 50, 51, 52 and 53

- Read together the story of the Good Shepherd on page 50 and discuss the "Something to Think About" questions. Then share the "Let us Pray" prayer on page 51.
- Read together the story of Zacchaeus on page 52. Ask your child how he or she thinks Zacchaeus felt after meeting Jesus. Go through each of the four ways to prepare for the sacrament of Reconciliation (page 53). Help your child memorize the prayer of contrition.

Pages 54 and 55

- Read and discuss these two pages. They describe the actual steps your child will take in celebrating the sacrament of Reconciliation. Assure your child that if he or she forgets something, the priest will help. You may want to review these pages several times before the sacrament so that your child is comfortable and above all not afraid.

Page 56

- Read this page with your child after he or she has celebrated First Reconciliation. Share the five questions in the middle of the page and, if you can recall them, share your own thoughts and feelings at your own First Reconciliation.
- Review the "Words to Remember" and ask your child to define them in his or her own words. End this time together by praying the "Let us Pray" prayer.

Suggestions for daily life

- Plan a special party with family and friends to celebrate your child's First Reconciliation. Ask guests to recall their own First Reconciliation and share these stories with your child.
- Remember to say "I'm sorry" when you make mistakes as a parent and remind your child to say "I'm sorry" to teachers, classmates, friends, and siblings when he or she does something wrong.

Enrichment activities

- Input or write all the "Words to Remember" from your child's book on separate slips of paper. Play a family game of "Can you guess?" by reading the definitions and letting family members name the words.
- If your parish schedules communal reconciliation services, attend as a family so your child can continue to celebrate the sacrament on a regular basis.

Conclusion

Congratulations and thank you for all you have done to make your child's celebration happen!

We hope that this special time with your child, especially your prayer moments and one-on-one conversations, has brought you closer together. We hope that the journey you have experienced here has been a wonderful and informative one for you and your child, bringing you even closer to Jesus, who is ever loving and forgiving.

You have journeyed with your child to his or her First Reconciliation. May you both continue to talk and pray and celebrate this sacrament together long after this first experience.

A simple celebration meal

In Preparation

- Invite your child to help prepare part of the meal, such as a special bread or dessert that everyone enjoys.
- Help your child write a short prayer expressing joy at celebrating the sacrament of Reconciliation.
- Decorate the dinner table. In the middle of the table place a large candle (if possible, your child's baptismal candle).

At the Meal

- At an appropriate moment, ask your child to bring the special bread or dessert to the table. Invite your child to read the prayer he or she wrote.
- Now ask your child to light the candle and invite the family to pray spontaneous prayers of thanksgiving and joy.

This Family Guide is an integral part of
We Prepare for Reconciliation—Child's Book.

Authors: Françoise Darcy-Berube and Jean-Paul Berube
Editors: Gwen Costello and Myrtle Power
Cover: Céleste Gagnon
Design & Layout: Céleste Gagnon
Photo credits: Anna Payne-Krzyzanowski: cover; p. 3: © Nic Neish/Shutterstock;
p. 4: © WP Wittman Photography; p. 5: © iStockphoto.com/Doug Schneider;
p. 6: © iStockphoto.com/MentalArt; p. 13: © Nic Neish/Shutterstock;
p. 14: © Jamie Wilson. Image from BigStockPhoto.com.
p. 15: © iStockphoto.com/Juan Gabriel Estey.
Illustrations: Anna Payne-Krzyzanowski: cover; June Bradford: p. 5, p. 16

© 2019 Novalis Publishing Inc.

NOVALIS
1 Eglinton Avenue East , Suite 800
Toronto, ON, Canada M4P 3A1
www.novalis.ca

TWENTY-THIRD
PUBLICATIONS
twentythirdpublications.com

Published in the United States by
Twenty-Third Publications
One Montauk Ave., Suite 200, New London, CT 06320
www.twentythirdpublications.com

When he taught the people, Jesus always spoke about God. He told them that his Father was always with him, and that's why he was so full of joy.

Many times, Jesus would go off by himself to find a quiet place to pray. When his friends looked for him, they often found him alone on a hillside talking to God.

Jesus' friends wanted to share his joy, so one day they said, "Lord, teach us how to pray." Jesus was happy to help them.

Something to Think About

- Why do you think Jesus wanted to be alone to pray?
- Have you ever felt the joy of being loved and forgiven?

From the Bible

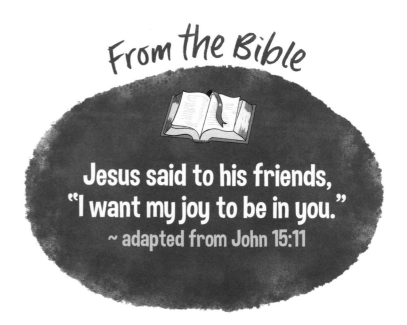

Jesus said to his friends, "I want my joy to be in you."
~ adapted from John 15:11

The Lord's Prayer

Here are the prayer words that Jesus gave his friends.
This prayer is also called the Our Father.

Our Father...

You are the Father of Jesus, but we, too, are your children. You know our names and love us very much. We can talk to you any time, the way we would talk to the most loving father or mother.

Who art in heaven...

Heaven is your home, the place of light where you live. But you also live in our hearts and you are always with us.

Hallowed be thy name...

When we say your name, God, we are speaking of the most wonderful being who exists. So we pray that your name will always be loved and respected by everyone.

Thy kingdom come...

Where you are in heaven, there is always joy. We ask that the same joy be in us. May we have this joy now, here on earth, and share it with others.

Thy will be done on earth as it is in heaven...

You know what is best for us. You always show us the right way. May we always follow your Law of Love.

Give us this day our daily bread...

We ask you, loving Father, for food to feed our bodies. We also ask that we may learn to share our food so that everyone in the world can have enough to eat. Please give us the kind of food we need to live your Law of Love.

And forgive us our trespasses as we forgive those who trespass against us...

It is often hard to forgive. But your forgiveness, God, cannot enter our hearts if we close them to others. Only you can teach us to forgive others and then to welcome your forgiveness.

And lead us not into temptation...

We say to you, "Lord, keep us walking on your path. Do not let us take paths that will lead us away from you."

But deliver us from evil...

Keep us away from all that can harm us. May we never bring harm to others.

Amen.

Yes, I believe all these things deep within my heart!

Learn the Our Father **by heart.** Remember that millions of people around the world say this prayer from Jesus.

The Church Teaches...

The Lord's prayer is truly the most perfect of prayers.
- adapted for children from CCC #2774

Many Ways to Pray

Jesus' joy came from being very close to God his Father. Talking to God helped keep his joy alive. Jesus wants to share his joy with us, and so he gives us a helper called the Holy Spirit to remind us to pray often. Here are some of the ways people pray with the help of the Holy Spirit.

Connor must hurry in the morning, but he always takes a few moments to say good morning to God.

Thank you, God, for this new day. Keep me safe and happy.

At Rosa and Mario's home, the family prays together before supper.

Bless us, O Lord, and these your gifts...

Simon is very angry because his friend was mean to him. He tries to calm down by talking to Jesus. Write what you think he is saying to Jesus.

Every week at Mass, we celebrate together with others in our parish because Jesus is with us. We sing together, pray together, and share the Lord's Supper together.

Therefore, O Lord, we humbly implore you: by the same Spirit graciously make holy these gifts we have brought to you for consecration, that they may become the Body and Blood of your Son our Lord Jesus Christ...

Learning About Quiet Prayer

There are many ways to pray. All of them bring great peace and joy. All of them bring us closer to God. Jesus often prayed in a quiet place.

If you would like to try **quiet prayer**, here's what you can do:

- Sit down facing your prayer corner or other quiet place.
- Close your eyes.
- Breathe slowly and deeply a few times until you feel quiet inside.
- Remember that Jesus is with you.
- In a very soft voice, or in your heart, slowly say a short prayer. Say it over and over, as often as you like. Some people say the name "Jesus" until the peace of God fills their hearts.
- Sit still for as long as you like and share with God whatever is in your heart.

From the Bible

Jesus, full of the Holy Spirit, was led into the wilderness to fast and pray.
~ adapted from Luke 4:1

Jesus, please be with me always. I want to follow your way.

Another way to pray is with your imagination.
Here's how to pray this way:

- Choose a favourite gospel story about Jesus. Read the story and then close your eyes.
- Picture Jesus and the other people in the story in your mind.
- Try to "see" how the people look and what they are doing.
- What sounds do you "hear"?
- What do you "smell"?
- Try to guess what the people are thinking and how they are feeling. Are they sad, happy, surprised?
- Now imagine that Jesus is speaking to you. What is he saying?
- Finish by speaking to Jesus in your own words.

When you pray, you are staying close to Jesus and his light shines through you. Those who pray often feel the joy of Jesus in their hearts.

Write what you think this boy is saying.

From the Bible

You are the light of the world. Let your light SHINE before others, so that they may SEE your good works and give glory to your Father in heaven.

~ adapted from Matthew 5:14-16

35

Mary's Prayer

Mary is Jesus' mother. She is our mother, too. She asks God to watch over each of us. Mary talked to God often when she was a young woman. One day, the angel Gabriel came to visit her. (An angel is one who brings a message from God.) Gabriel told Mary that God wanted her to be the mother of Jesus. Mary said, "Yes, I will do whatever God asks of me."

The Church has a special prayer to Mary called the **Hail Mary**. Millions of Catholics all over the world pray this prayer every day! You can pray it as often as you like. Invite your family to pray it with you.

Let us Pray

Learn this prayer by heart.

Hail Mary, full of grace,
the Lord is with you.

Blessed are you among women
and blessed is the fruit of
your womb, Jesus.

Holy Mary, Mother of God,
pray for us sinners,
now and at the hour
of our death.
Amen.

3. What Have You Learned?

God gives us the wonderful gift of joy, a feeling of happiness deep within our hearts. Jesus had this gift. He wants us to have it, too. We have joy in a special way when we pray.

Answer these questions in your own words.

1. **What made Jesus so happy in his life?**

_____

2. **How can you share in his joy?**

_____

3. **Who did God send to help us pray?**

_____

How to keep God's joy in your heart:

- Talk to God every morning and every evening.
- Talk to Jesus in your heart often during the day.
- Take time for quiet prayer. Ask your family to join you sometimes.
- Take good care of your prayer corner. Put up drawings, pictures, or Bible words that will help you pray.
- Pray the Our Father often, alone and with your family. This prayer is so special to the Church, we pray it every Sunday at Mass.

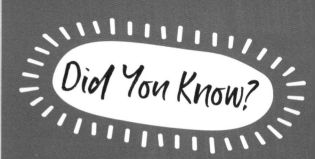

Did You Know?

Every time you go to Mass, you pray the Lord's Prayer. Next time, listen well, and when the prayer begins, join in with a loud, clear voice.

Words to Remember...

Joy ~ a feeling of happiness that comes from knowing that God loves you

The Lord's Prayer ~ The prayer Jesus taught his followers. It is also called the Our Father.

By heart ~ to remember, to keep something in your mind

Quiet prayer ~ a way to pray without using many words

Prayer of imagination ~ a way to pray with Bible stories using your imagination

Mary ~ the mother of Jesus who prays for us always

37

4. God Gives You Peace

Everyone wants to be happy and get along with others. We all like to feel peaceful and happy. That's what God wants for us, too. This is God's great dream, the dream that Jesus came to tell us about: "Stay close to God and God's plan for you, and you will have peace and joy in your life."

From the Bible

Have mercy on me, O God, because I am weak and I have sinned.

~ adapted from Psalm 106:6

But sometimes things happen and we turn away from God's love. Whether we are children or grown-ups, we may do or say things to others that hurt them.

- We take something that is not ours.
- We cheat or we lie.
- We disobey our parents or teachers.
- We hurt other people's feelings.

To say this in another way, we choose **sin**.

When we sin, we cause pain and suffering instead of peace and happiness.

Here are some stories about what happens when we turn away from God.

When You Disobey

Amelia and her mom have just moved to a new house. Amelia's grandparents are coming to see it. There is a lot of work to do before they arrive. Amelia's mom has to hang up some curtains and then prepare a special supper.

But once Amelia gets outside...

Something to Think About

- Why did Amelia disobey her mother?
- Did her actions hurt anyone?
- Do you think Amelia followed God's Law of Love?

When You Hurt Others

Caleb got a remote-control car for his birthday. All the kids really liked it.

Later, James noticed that Caleb had left his car in the cloakroom.

Something to Think About

- Why would James do something like this to his friend?
- How do you think James felt about it?
- Do you think James was following God's dream for him?

No one was around, so James took the car.

At the end of the day, Caleb couldn't find his car. He asked his friends about it.

Has anyone seen my car?

No, I haven't seen it since recess.

When Stephanie tries to read, all the letters look mixed up.

Yesterday, the teacher asked her to read out loud in class. She made mistakes right away.

The ... um ... horses ... um ... wall ... walked ... um ...

She should go back to first grade.

Behind her, Lydia and Christine started making fun of her. Stephanie heard them. She stopped reading and started to cry.

She can't even read a sentence!

In God's Law of Love, there is no place for sin. When you do wrong, you hurt yourself and others. God loves you and wants you to be happy. God wants you to turn away from sin.

Something to Think About

- Is it okay to make fun of someone? Why or why not?
- How do you feel when someone makes fun of you?
- Do you think Lydia and Christine were following God's dream for them?

43

God Always Guides You

Did you know? God has placed a small voice inside you that helps you know what is right or wrong. This voice is called your **conscience**. In the Bible, God gives rules that help your conscience make good choices. These are called the **Ten Commandments**. They are mostly for grown-ups, but you can learn them, too. In the gospels, Jesus gives us rules that will keep us on the path to God and help our **conscience** to learn God's Law of Love. We call these rules **gospel teachings**.

The Ten Commandments

1. **Love God with all your heart.**
2. **Do not curse or swear.**
3. **Remember that Sunday is a holy day.**
4. **Love and respect your parents.**
5. **Respect all life.**
6. **Be a good and faithful husband or wife.**
7. **Do not steal from others.**
8. **Do not tell lies.**
9. **Do not be jealous of what others have.**
10. **Respect your neighbours and all that is theirs.**

– adapted from Exodus 20:1-21

Rules from Jesus

1. Do not be angry with your brother or sister.
2. Keep your promises.
3. If anyone hits you, don't hit back.
4. Don't worry. God will take care of you.
5. If someone is hungry, share food with them.
6. Give to everyone who asks for your help.
7. If someone wants to borrow something from you, be generous.
8. Love your enemies and pray for those who hurt you.

All of these are important, but here is Jesus' greatest rule:

Love one another as I have loved you.

~ all adapted from the Gospels.

Jesus also said, "Be **perfect** as your heavenly Father is perfect." (Matthew 5:48) That's another way of saying: "Live God's Law of Love in everything you do." It takes great courage to follow your conscience and do the right thing. But when you do, you are following the path to love and joy, to peace and reconciliation. In other words, you are following the path to God.

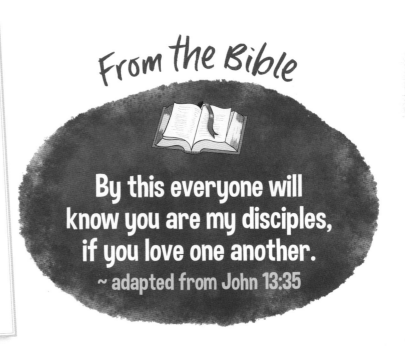

From the Bible

By this everyone will know you are my disciples, if you love one another.
~ adapted from John 13:35

God Always Forgives You

Jesus teaches that when we have sinned, we should always return to God our Father because God never stops loving us. Many times during his life, Jesus forgave people who had sinned. He asked them to return to God's Law of Love.

One day some people brought a woman to Jesus. She had been caught doing something very wrong. They wanted Jesus to punish her. Instead, he forgave the woman and told her to sin no more.

Jesus was very kind to sinners. He welcomed them with so much love that many people were very surprised. God our Father acts in the same way with us. God even gives us a special sign of forgiveness. It is the sacrament of Reconciliation.

It's true. We all do bad things sometimes and we need to be forgiven. Think of a time when someone you love forgave you.

- How did you feel before you were forgiven? Were you sorry you had done wrong?

- What did you do or say to show you were sorry?

- How did you feel after you were forgiven? Why?

Let us Pray

Dear God,
please give me courage
so I always do
the right thing.

When I make a mistake
and hurt someone,
help me to say I'm sorry.

God Invites You to Change

God forgives us with love when we are truly sorry for our sins. But God also wants us to ask those we have hurt to forgive us. God wants us to change the way we treat others.

Read the stories on pages 40, 41, 42, and 43 one more time. How could the children make up for what they did?

What do you think?

- How could Amelia make up for disobeying her mother?

- How could James make up for stealing from Caleb and lying to him?

- How could Lydia and Christine make up for hurting Stephanie?

4. What Have You Learned?

You are now getting closer to the day when you will celebrate the sacrament of Reconciliation for the first time. Can you remember some of the things you have learned?

1. When you do something wrong on purpose,

    this is called a ____ ____ ____ .

2. God does not want you to sin, because

    when you do, you ____ ____ ____ ____ others and yourself, too.

3. God is always ready to f ____ r g ____ ____ ____ you

    because God never stops l ____ v ____ ____ ____ you.

4. We can tell right from wrong because God has given us a

    c ____ ____ scie ____ ____ ____ .

5. One of the ways we form our conscience is by remembering the

    ____ ____ ____ C ____ mm ____ ____ ____ ments.

6. Another way is by remembering Jesus'

    t ____ ____ ____ ____ ings in the gospels.

(Check your answers at the bottom of the page.)

Words to Remember...

Sin ~ an action we do on purpose that turns us away from God and hurts others

Ten Commandments ~ laws that God gave to the Jewish people

Gospel teachings ~ guidelines or rules that Jesus gave us to stay close to God

Conscience ~ a small inner voice that God placed in our hearts to help us know right from wrong

Being "perfect" ~ living God's Law of Love

ANSWERS: 1. sin 2. hurt 3. forgive, loving 4. conscience 5. Ten Commandments 6. teachings

5. God Gives You Forgiveness

For a few weeks, you have been learning about God's Law of Love. Now it is time to think about God's forgiveness. Let's start with a beautiful story from Jesus.

Once upon a time, there was a shepherd who had 100 sheep. He loved them very much and took good care of them. One evening, as he led the sheep back to their pen, he counted them as usual: 97, 98, 99... But where was the last one?

The worried shepherd left his other sheep and ran off to find the lost one. At last he found her at the bottom of the hill. She was stuck in a thorn bush.

Did he get mad at her? Not at all. He was so happy that he put her on his shoulders and sang to her all the way home. As he passed through the village, he invited everyone he saw to celebrate with him.

Come celebrate with me! I found my lost sheep.

Something to Think About

- How did this story make you feel?
- Jesus calls himself the Good Shepherd. How is he like the shepherd in the story?
- What does this story say to you about God's love and forgiveness?

The sacrament of Reconciliation is like this story. Jesus is the shepherd who leads us to God. When we turn away from God through sin, we are like the lost sheep. When we turn our hearts once again to God, it's time for a happy **celebration**. Jesus rejoices when we stay on the path to God.

Remember that sin is something we do on purpose that turns us away from God and hurts others. Anytime we turn away from God through sin, we must find a way to turn back to God.

From the Bible

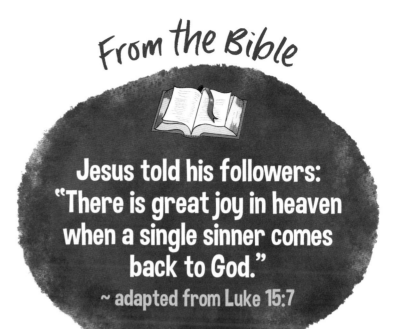

Jesus told his followers: "There is great joy in heaven when a single sinner comes back to God."

~ adapted from Luke 15:7

Let us Pray

O Lord Jesus, you are my good shepherd.
You are always with me, so I will not be afraid.
Thank you for keeping me on the path to God.
Amen.

A Story of Forgiveness

Very soon you will celebrate the sacrament of Reconciliation. You will meet with a priest who will welcome you with joy. He will offer you forgiveness in Jesus' name. This story will help you understand what happens in the sacrament.

There once was a man named Zacchacus who really wanted to see Jesus. Zacchaeus was too short to see over the crowd, so he climbed a tree. When Jesus saw him there, he said, "Zacchaeus, I think I'll come to your house for lunch today." Zacchaeus was a tax collector and the people hated him. They called him a sinner.

But Zacchaeus listened carefully to Jesus and what he said about God's Law of Love. He knew that he had taken the wrong path and had sinned. He spoke to Jesus about it because he could tell that Jesus loved him.

Jesus forgave Zacchaeus for all his sins. At the end of the meal, Zacchaeus thanked Jesus and told him how happy he was.

Preparing for the Sacrament

During the week before your First Reconciliation, spend time each day remembering Jesus and his message. This is the best way to prepare for the sacrament of Reconciliation.

1. **Remember how much Jesus loves you.** He invites you to follow him on the path to God. When you say yes to this invitation, you will find great joy, just as Zacchaeus did.

2. **Pray to Jesus through quiet prayer.** Close your eyes and picture Jesus sitting with you at lunch. Talk to him about the sacrament of Reconciliation. Are you nervous about it? Are you looking forward to it? Share whatever is in your heart.

3. **Remember your sins.** Think about Jesus and God's Law of Love. Do you live it in all your words and actions? Do you pray every day? Do you sometimes hurt others by making fun of them, by fighting, by stealing from them, or by lying to them? Do you sometimes disobey your parents on purpose? Do you ever refuse to help someone in need, to share with them, or to forgive them?

4. **Ask for God's forgiveness.** In your own words, tell God you are sorry for your sins. Or use this prayer:

O my God, I am sorry with
all my heart for doing wrong.
I love you and do not want to sin again.
You are all good and deserving of all my love.
I will try with your help to sin no more.
Amen.

**Try to learn this prayer by heart
so you can use it during the sacrament
of Reconciliation.**

Celebrating Reconciliation

When you meet with the priest for the sacrament of Reconciliation, you will follow a few simple steps that lead to joy and forgiveness. You do not need to remember them all. If you forget something, the priest will help you.

- First, the priest welcomes you with joy. Greet him and then make the Sign of the Cross together.

- Next, the priest will read to you from the Bible. The Bible is the book of God's Word, and a sign of God's living presence among us. God will be with you as you celebrate this sacrament.

- Now you tell the priest about times you have done wrong on purpose and hurt other people in some way. Speak to him as you would speak to Jesus. The priest will NEVER tell anyone else what you say. The priest will ask you to make up for your sins by doing a special action or saying a prayer.

This is called your **penance**. It shows that you want to get back on the path to God.

- Now you tell God through the priest that you are sorry for your sins. You can use the prayer on page 53. The priest then offers you God's forgiveness with these words of **absolution**: "I absolve you from your sins in the name of the Father, and of the Son, and of the Holy Spirit." These words are the sign that God forgives you and is giving you a fresh start. At the end you answer, "Amen."

- The last step is to give thanks to God by saying a prayer of praise and sharing the greeting of peace. Then you thank the priest and leave the reconciliation room. Make sure to do or say the penance the priest has given you. Some people like to do their penance right away so they don't forget!

5. What Have You Learned?

Congratulations! You have made the journey to the sacrament of Reconciliation. Take a moment to think about this journey. Read page 6 in this book again.

Then think about these questions:
- What did you enjoy most on this journey?
- Was it hard sometimes? Why?
- Do you understand now how to stay close to God by living God's Law of Love?
- How did it feel to talk to the priest?
- How does it feel to have all your sins forgiven?

Now, like the children on this page, you can continue walking the path of God with Jesus. May you always enjoy God's gifts of life, love, joy, peace, and forgiveness!

Words to Remember...

Good shepherd ~ one who really loves and cares for the sheep. Jesus is our Good Shepherd because he cares for each one of us.

Celebration ~ a time to be happy and give thanks to God

Penance ~ a special action or prayer that shows you are truly sorry for your sins

Absolution ~ the words of forgiveness that the priest uses in the sacrament of Reconciliation

Let us Pray

I thank you, God of Love,
with all my heart
for all the gifts
you have given me.
With Jesus' help,
I'll walk with you always.

Amen.